WONE   ~~~ ~~
STUDY OF THEOLOGY

A MEDITATION FOR SEMINARIANS

JOHN GRESHAM, PH.D.

THOMAS NEAL, PH.D.

THE INSTITUTE FOR PRIESTLY FORMATION

IPF PUBLICATIONS

THE INSTITUTE FOR PRIESTLY FORMATION
IPF Publications
2500 California Plaza
Omaha, Nebraska 68178
www.IPFPublications.com

Printed in the United States of America
ISBN-13: 978-0-9981164-3-3

Cover design by Timothy D. Boatright
Marketing Associates, USA
Tampa, Florida

THE INSTITUTE FOR PRIESTLY FORMATION

Mission Statement

The Institute for Priestly Formation was founded to assist bishops in the spiritual formation of diocesan seminarians and priests in the Roman Catholic Church. The Institute responds to the need to foster spiritual formation as the integrating and governing principle of all aspects for priestly formation. Inspired by the biblical-evangelical spirituality of Ignatius Loyola, this spiritual formation has as its goal the cultivation of a deep interior communion with Christ; from such communion, the priest shares in Christ's own pastoral charity. In carrying out its mission, the Institute directly serves diocesan seminarians and priests as well as those who are responsible for diocesan priestly formation.

THE INSTITUTE FOR PRIESTLY FORMATION
Creighton University
2500 California Plaza
Omaha, Nebraska 68178
www.priestlyformation.org
ipf@creighton.edu

TABLE OF CONTENTS

FOREWORD

It is our hope that these two inspiring essays will be a gift to seminarians to be read with each new academic year. The authors, two seasoned seminary theologians and academic deans, encourage the hearts of seminarians to anchor their study in the Spirit, in wonder, and in the living truths that theology endeavors to prayerfully and rigorously explore.

Seminary is a unique gift to Western culture and does not seek to simply repeat the mission of the university. This uniqueness is found in the very words of Christ Himself, "I have called you friends" (Jn 15:15). How does a friend *know* a friend? We know a friend by progressive assimilation. The seminary classroom is an appropriate setting for a man to come to know God in such a way. Knowing in this way invites the vocation itself to be the driving force of study. The seminarian approaches the study of theology as the content of the life to which he aspires. A seminary, unlike a secularized university, orders academic study not solely from a disposition of skepticism or critique, but sees study as a search for Truth *from within the friendship* the seminarian has with Christ.

Certainly, criticism is part of an appropriate classroom method; but primarily, we approach the doctrinal tradition in faith, hope, and love. The study of theology always involves a person undergoing conversion to God and not simply mastering an academic discipline. Seminarians want their theological study to affect them and move them toward intellectual competency and contemplative rest.

As the *Program of Priestly Formation* describes: "The first task of intellectual formation is to acquire a personal knowledge of the Lord Jesus Christ . . . This saving knowledge is acquired not only once, but it is continuously appropriated and deepened. . . . this knowledge is not simply for personal possession but is destined to be shared in the community of faith."[1] Each seminary needs to find its way of ordering the men in formation toward a personal appropriation of Christ living His mysteries over again within them.

In so doing, the seminary develops seminarians who emerge from formation as spiritual leaders, drawing parishioners into the unfolding mysteries of Christ. These mysteries, however, had to be first received by the seminarian in his acceptance of an integrated life of worship, study, human growth, and charity that is seminary.

A seminary is a school, but it is a school that explores the science of *the Person who is The Christ.* This Person, as Cardinal Newman taught, is worthy of objective study but also of praise and adoration. Newman's goal for theology was to integrate intellect and devotion. He rejects pious sentimentalism, as he does rationalism. Instead, he strives to cultivate the "the practice of the saintly intellect."[2] The following meditations, which I would encourage be read in the opening days of each new formation year in seminary, carry us into that practice.

Deacon James Keating, Ph.D.
Director of Theological Formation
The Institute for Priestly Formation
Creighton University; Omaha, Nebraska

NOTES

1.   United States Conference of Catholic Bishops (USCCB), *Program of Priestly Formation*, 5th ed. (Washington DC: USCCB, 2006), sec. 137.

2.   John H. Newman, *On Consulting the Faithful in Matters of Doctrine* (New York: Sheed & Ward, 1961), 48.

THEOLOGIANS KEEPING
WONDER ALIVE

THOMAS J. NEAL

Every fall, as I resume a new academic year, I ask myself the question: How can I keep alive the fires of Pentecost, the free-falling Spirit of God who has kindled in my heart a new song? The same Spirit kindles and flares up in your hearts as well. Especially, I am thinking here of your seminary intellectual formation.

For me, the word "wonder" captures the *genius of contemplative theology*.

Studying theology is meant to be more than cerebral acrobatics. It is an exploration, a quest, a plunge into and—to use an image from St. John of the Cross—a *hunt* for God in which we discover a very disconcerting fact: It is actually God who is pursuing us, hunting us. And when He finally captures us,

He is the one who is slaughtered to become for us a feast, a life-giving feast in which He gives us Himself as food for the journey.

Theology allows us the chance to peer into the mind of this pursuing God, Jesus Christ—and there, deep in the fiery abyss of His Heart, we discover what He has been thinking about all along: " . . . us men and our salvation," as the Creed says it. That is what preoccupies His thoughts—us, and our well-being. My God.

Studying theology is nothing other than a living entry of our mind into the mind of the ascending Christ through the energetic Paschal Spirit,[1] a progressive synergy of thoughts. Thinking, not simply about, but *into* each other. When we enter Christ's beautiful mind, we find ourselves thinking about very "priestly" things—what Jesus thinks of always: the salvation and well-being of all.

And you suddenly see that your sweaty virtues, your every hard labor in study and prayer, in your daily asceticism and apostolic service are all but a single, proleptic, forward-looking labor of love— already now, before you are ordained, you *are* loving *God's people*. And loving God's people is the highest form of love for God a priest can have in this life.

"Simon son of John, do you love me? . . . Feed my lambs . . . Tend my sheep . . . Feed my sheep" (Jn 21:15-17).

And when we learn to study and think in prayer,[2] we become not just talking heads but mystagogues who lead others into the Great Mysteries, the mind and heart of Christ, the God who loved mankind into the very bowels of hell.

I have been studying theology in an academic way since the Fall of 1987 when I took my first Scripture class, and have worked within the institutional Church for twenty-six years—I have seen wonder live, and I have seen wonder die. I would like to say a few words about keeping wonder alive . . . what it looks like to stay in love as theologians fully alive in Christ.

The greatest teachers, preachers, and leaders I have known in my life—who inspire me and others—have, without exception, been people filled with a contagious, irrepressible wonder.

There is nothing worse than a teacher, a priest, a spouse, or a parent who has lost his or her sense of wonder and been consumed by bitterness, cynicism, pettiness, a critical soul grown shallow, laced with a black and toxic humor.

Wonder is bright and life-giving. It lifts up the heart and is encouraging. It is filled with joy and is generous with its vitality.

Wonder is a hunger to know, to learn; it is the capacity to be surprised, amazed, astonished. It is the antidote to boredom, apathy, and the self-reliant need to be in control of everything. It is the openness to see everything anew again and again, like the child who, alone, Jesus says, can enter the Kingdom of God. It is the disposition to see in all creation, everything around you—from the tiniest flower to the soaring cathedral, from the dying cancer victim to the weeping widow—to see all things in the light of the life-giving Cross, as an epiphany of a provident God who is at every moment making all things new. Wonder is the ability to see everything— absolutely everything—as pure gift, unmerited, undeserved, gratuitously given. And so, wonder gives birth to gratitude.

Wonder's disposition of constant surprise and fascination filled the great theologian saints, like St. Albert the Great. It is said that as he would travel on foot with his fellow itinerant Dominican friars, he would wander constantly off the beaten path into the fields and hedges and forests to explore the menagerie of plants and insects and rocks and snakes . . . and would sing the Canticle of Daniel, calling all creation to "bless the Lord." A true priest of creation.

Or wonder is like my daughter Catherine who, when she was four, was downstairs in our basement sitting next to a lovely antique table. We had a rule in the house: no shoes inside to prevent mud from being tracked in. So when I came downstairs one afternoon and found her sitting at that table, a bucket of mud next to her, and piles of mud on top of the table, I *lost* it. I yelled: "*What are you doing*?!" Her eyes welled up with big, hot tears and her lower lip trembled. She said, in a trembling voice: "B-b-but Daddy, I was j-just building us a castle to live in together."

I fell to my knees next to her, in such joy, overwhelmed by the revelation of her secret intention. I said, in repentance, "Oh, I am so sorry. Yes! Beautiful! Let me help you!"

My love for her, her love for me opened my eyes to see in that mess, that mud, that "sin," a beauty, a wonder, a love. A castle.

Love rewrites the world.

Wonder made a physicist I studied under, who was also a devout Orthodox Jew, blurt out in the middle of his lecture to bored young college students: "How can you all be bored, when all around you is a world that didn't have to exist at all, but does? Something rather than nothing—that's enough to get me stuck on 'wow' for a thousand years!"

It was the wonder, born of faith in Christ crucified, that kept Maximilian Kolbe from despair in the starvation bunker at Auschwitz; wonder that—as eyewitnesses later testified—filled that bunker with song, with hope; and wonder that gave Kolbe the kind and loving eyes that made his medical executioner order him blindfolded before he injected him with carbolic acid.

It was wonder that shaped my paternal grandfather, who died at one week shy of one hundred years old—who was orphaned at the age of six, dropped out of high school but later put himself through Brown University and became a successful business executive. Wonder filled both his and my grandmother's seventy-eight years of faithful married life. A scrappy, street smart boxer with cauliflower ear, my grandfather hungered and thirsted for knowledge; he was a voracious reader, a dilettante who learned a bit of everything from anyone and everyone. He listened far more than he spoke.

He was a realist to the core, but hope filled, faith filled. He never criticized anyone, except to the person's face; and he never cursed, saying vulgar language was a sign of an impoverished vocabulary and a shallow soul. Language, he said, is man's most ennobling gift.

He was a man who, when you left his presence, made you feel more human, more hopeful . . . A man who wrote me seventeen handwritten letters, which I have saved, and one of which said: "Tommy, when you can see the Hand of God everywhere, you can learn from anyone and anything; always be learning and listening and watching and being surprised."

Wonder is, of course, above all, found in Christ. Stay close to Him, the supremely wonder-filled Man, and you will never grow weary.

Once, in a public lecture, I heard Fr. Thomas Hopko, my favorite Orthodox public intellectual, say:

On the Cross, powerless, stripped, rejected, naked, bleeding and dying, God, who is all-powerful, all-just, all-holy, perfectly innocent and pure, who could in an instant annihilate the entire cosmos with a word, whom man cannot even look on without dying, who was offended and blasphemed and rejected by our sins—this God in essence says to us from that Cross: I don't want to hurt you. I want to raise you, restore you, redeem you, reconcile you.

Wonder gives you a window into *that* world; it stays alive even as you find yourself in the valley of the shadow of death.

Let me end here with the words of an African Methodist Episcopal (AME) pastor in Tallahassee, Florida, where I used to live. He invited me to his church for a Wednesday evening worship service.

Because he knew I was coming, he decided to preach on the Last Supper. It was awesome.

He knew how to preach. A deep, raspy, sing-songy voice that exuded passion and faith. There was an electric moment in his forty-five-minute-long sermon that night, as he commented on Jesus' words, "Take, Eat." The pastor said, with that amazing voice:

To git it you gotta take it;
to take it you gotta want it;
to want it you gotta be hungry
and if ya ain't hungry
ya ain't ever gonna git it. Got it?

Stay hungry, my dear brothers. You have fallen in love. Now, stay in love. Amen.

NOTES

1. Jean Corbon, *The Wellspring of Worship* (San Francisco: Ignatius Press, 1988).

2. James Keating, "Theology as Thinking in Prayer," *Chicago Studies* (Spring 2014) 53.1: 70.

BUILDING BRIDGES: INTEGRATING INTELLECTUAL AND SPIRITUAL FORMATION

JOHN GRESHAM

The *Program of Priestly Formation* describes the four areas of formation—human, spiritual, intellectual, and pastoral—but emphasizes that all four must be integrated with one another. The description of each dimension of formation concludes with a paragraph describing how that area of formation is related to the other three. Human formation provides the foundation for spiritual, intellectual, and pastoral formation.[1] Spiritual formation is the heart and center around which the other three areas are integrated.[2] Intellectual formation develops human intelligence (human formation), leads to spiritual understanding of the ways of God (spiritual formation), and prepares men to share the mystery of faith with others (pastoral formation).[3] Pastoral formation is the goal that integrates all formation in service toward others.[4]

Compartmentalization

Seminaries strive to implement the *Program of Priestly Formation's* emphasis on integration; but despite their best efforts, such integration does not come about easily. The seminarian will find himself pulled away from integration toward its opposite: compartmentalization. Rather than integrating human, spiritual, intellectual, and pastoral formation, the seminarian will be tempted to divide his life in such a way that each area of formation occupies its own independent "compartment" within his busy life. Even the seminary itself, in its communal and institutional expression, must fight the temptation to compartmentalize each dimension of formation into its own structure with its own specialized staff and processes—that is, formation advisers exclusively dealing with human formation; spiritual directors exclusively providing spiritual formation; academic faculty exclusively doing intellectual formation.

Compartmentalization is the great temptation of our modern age. It is how we deal with the complexities of modern life. Modern persons are tempted to cope with these complexities by neatly dividing (or attempting to divide) their lives into separate compartments: family, work, leisure, and (in some safe place, where it will not inconvenience the rest) spiritual life. We each must struggle against this tendency toward compartmentalization and cry for the Holy Spirit to unify each area of our life around our identity in Christ as beloved children of the Father.

This struggle, so characteristic of life in a secularized society, does not disappear in the seminary. In fact, the seminarian often finds himself even more tempted toward compartmentalization as a means of surviving the challenges of living in the "hothouse" of seminary formation. As a survival tactic, the seminarian switches into "intellectual" mode when he sits in the classroom; focuses on his "spiritual" life when speaking to his spiritual director; puts on his "pastoral" persona as he goes out on apostolic assignment; and then tries simply to be "human" with his formation adviser or, perhaps, hanging out with his brother seminarians.

To combat this inevitable compartmentalization are some simple practices that build bridges between different areas of formation. As the seminarian finds himself dividing his formation (and his life) into separate compartments, he needs to build bridges to connect (or re-connect) what has become separated. These bridges become the instruments of integration. Rather than focusing on all four areas of formation, this essay provides examples of building bridges between intellectual formation and spiritual formation. This is a crucial area of integration because the classroom and study take up so much of the seminarian's time and energy that it is easy to separate those things from the other areas of formation, especially the spiritual life. Moreover, the *Program of Priestly Formation* gives special attention to the importance of integrating these two specific areas of formation: "there is a reciprocal relationship between spiritual and intellectual formation. The intellectual life nourishes the spiritual life, but the spiritual life also opens vistas of understanding."[5] A more thorough integration of intellectual and spiritual formation—linking study and prayer, uniting head and heart—facilitates the integration of the other dimensions of formation: supporting deeper human transformation and fostering richer pastoral development.

Building Bridges Between Lectio Divina and Exegesis

One area where compartmentalization commonly occurs is the division between the personal meditation on Scripture in prayer (*lectio divina*) and the academic study of Scripture in the classroom (exegesis). A seminarian can spend a holy hour praying and meditating on a biblical text and then simply leave his meditations behind as he opens up the commentaries and begins to exegete the text for his Scripture class—or vice versa, what he has learned about the text in his Scripture class fails to enter into his prayer.

This separation is not only a problem in the seminary classroom. The guild of biblical scholarship has often been hampered by a rigid separation between the academic study of the biblical text and its reception by people of faith. New attention to theological interpretation and reception studies among biblical scholars has begun to bridge this divide. Yet, there is still the need to hear Pope Benedict XVI's warning of the "serious risk nowadays of a dualistic approach to sacred Scripture . . . a sterile separation . . . between exegesis and theology . . . a profound gulf . . . between scientific exegesis and Lectio Divina."[6] Some Biblical scholars are tempted to reduce Scripture study to a mere academic exercise of human reason apart from the illumination of faith. They might dismiss a practice like *lectio divina* as too subjective, thereby closing themselves off from a personal encounter with God in His Word.

Some seminarians (probably many) are tempted in the opposite direction. They have experienced the powerful presence of God and heard the voice of the Holy Spirit speaking to them as they prayerfully meditated on the words of Scripture. They accept *lectio divina* but dismiss the academic study of Scripture. The rationalistic excesses of some biblical scholars have soured them to the entire enterprise of historical criticism and literary analysis of Scripture. They learn just enough to satisfy their Biblical Studies professors but plan to leave that knowledge behind as soon as they are ordained! However, in doing this, they close themselves off from the deeper insights into the biblical message that such study can provide. Pope Benedict XVI emphasized the irreplaceable role of historical-critical methods as a requirement rooted in the historical character of Divine revelation itself. This method is "an indispensable dimension of exegetical work" because "it is of the very essence of biblical faith to be about real historical events."[7]

Seminarians need to experience how the academic study of Scripture can illumine their prayerful meditation on biblical texts. They need to take their exegesis, their study of the biblical text in the classroom, the insights gained from biblical commentaries and dictionaries, and bring that knowledge into their prayer. Conversely, they need to allow the insights received in *lectio divina* to draw them toward deeper exegesis of the text, to more profound and rigorous study of the text using all the exegetical tools available to them. To foster these experiences,

I invite seminarians to begin the following two practices as a simple way of building bridges between
lectio divina and exegesis: *lectio*-inspired exegesis and
exegetically informed *lectio*.

Lectio-Inspired Exegesis

In *lectio divina*, the seminarian is taught to slowly,
prayerfully, and repetitively read through a biblical text with an openness to the Holy Spirit. He is
encouraged to be attentive to the movements of
his heart and to notice and pause on that word or
phrase that most draws him out of himself toward
the Lord. He is to meditate and to pray with that
word or phrase and to be receptive to God's voice
until he rests in silent contemplation. The seminarian
might use his imagination to enter into the biblical
story and encounter the Lord there. Seminarians
often conclude their *lectio* by writing some insights
into a prayer journal and reflecting on those insights
through the day. I suggest seminarians take that
insight and build a bridge between *lectio* and exegesis
by *lectio*-inspired exegesis.

I am not suggesting the student write a lengthy
biblical research paper! Rather, I suggest the seminarian just take a moment to follow up some insights
from *lectio* by using some biblical research resource
to gain additional insight into that biblical text. The
seminarian can take that key word or passage he

received in prayer and spend just a few moments to learn more about it. If he is in the library, the seminarian might take just a moment to stop in the reference area of the library and look up his word in a Bible dictionary or grab a commentary and look up that passage; or he might use some of the online biblical studies tools to find some information. Over time, as he experiences how insights from his *lectio* are deepened through a bit of biblical research, the seminarian might build his own small collection of biblical reference works that he has found helpful.

One personal example of this method was when I was praying with a passage in Isaiah 44 where God promises to pour out His Spirit. Those who are to receive the Spirit are compared to two trees (Isaiah 44:4). The names of these plants vary among English translations of the Bible, but the New Revised Standard Version I was reading names them as the willow and the tamarisk. I knew the first tree but not the second. Later in the day, I simply took a moment to look up "tamarisk" in a Bible dictionary and learned that it is a tree that grows in arid soil (unlike the willow, which grows where there is water). Part of my meditation had been around receiving the Spirit "on dry ground" (Isaiah 44:3) and with this new information, I took this tamarisk tree as a symbol of the fruit that the Spirit could produce even in the dry soil of my heart and the hearts of others for whom I was praying.

Exegetically Informed Lectio Divina

This movement from *lectio divina* to exegesis (*lectio-inspired* exegesis) is complemented by the opposite movement from exegesis to *lectio* (exegetically informed *lectio divina*). As with *lectio divina*, when the seminarian listens to the professor lecture on a biblical passage or reads an interpretation of the passage in his text book, he should be open to the Spirit and attentive to the movements of his heart. If something in that passage moves his heart, the seminarian can make a little note to the side of his regular classroom notes. Here is something he wants to return to in prayer. As he goes to *lectio divina*, the seminarian takes up that word or passage that was illumined for him in a classroom lecture, a reading assignment, or his own exegetical research and lets it become the subject matter of his prayer and meditation, the content of his dialogue with the Lord. He takes what he has learned from an academic study of the passage—insights gained from a historical or literary exegesis of the text—and allows the Spirit to personalize those insights through prayer and meditation.

Again, by way of personal example, I had time for a little bit of further research on Isaiah 44 in addition to learning about the tamarisk tree. I did not spend much time, but I took a moment to look up the chapter in a couple of commentaries. Among other insights, I learned that "Jeshuron," the name used for Israel in this passage, was something like a term of endearment. I took my newfound exegetical insights with me as I returned to the passage in my daily *lectio* and prayer. Re-reading those verses with a sense of God's tender love expressed in this intimate "nickname" with which He addressed His beloved people led me into a deeper experience of God's love in my meditation.

Pope Francis on Exegesis, Lectio, and Preaching

If a seminarian begins to build bridges from personal meditation on Scripture to research—and from research to prayer and meditation—the pay-off from accumulated small increments of time will be the cultivation of a habit of linking prayer to study, and study to prayer. The seminarian will begin to habitually link his personal reception of Scripture to its linguistic, historical, and theological meanings and to interiorize that meaning through personal prayer. Beyond seminary, his preaching of God's Word will be enhanced by this integration of *lectio* and exegesis.

In *Evangelii Gaudium*, Pope Francis describes this integration of exegesis and lectio in homily preparation. He exhorts homilists to begin by giving full attention to the Biblical text, to attend to the meaning of the key words (in the original languages) and a literary analysis of the intent and purpose of the author. Next, he encourages a canonical reading of the text, interpreting the passage in relation to the teaching of the entire Bible.[8] Following that exegetical study of the text, Pope Francis then encourages the homilist to enter into the text through *lectio divina*. He quotes John Paul II's words from *Pastores Dabo Vobis*: "Knowledge of its linguistic or exegetical aspects, though certainly necessary is not enough. He needs to approach the word with a docile and prayerful heart so that it may deeply penetrate his thoughts and feelings and bring about a new outlook in him."[9] Pope Francis concludes by emphasizing how *lectio* and exegesis work together as the homilist listens to the Word in order to proclaim that Word to God's people. "This prayerful reading of the Bible is not something separate from the study undertaken by the preacher to ascertain the central message of the text; on the contrary, it should begin with that study and then go on to discern how that same message speaks to his own heart."[10]

Building Bridges between Doxology and Dogma

In addition to taking Scripture classes, the seminarian takes many classes in Dogmatic Theology (sometimes called Systematic Theology). As he may do with Scripture classes, the seminarian will be tempted to compartmentalize his academic study of dogmas (the mysteries of faith) and to separate that study from his experience of those same mysteries of faith in doxology (worship, Liturgy, personal prayer). He may spend an hour meditating in awe on the Mystery of the Incarnation as he sits in adoration of the Blessed Sacrament and then sit and yawn in boredom as his professor analyzes that very same mystery in the classroom! This is not always the fault of the seminarian. We faculty, trained in an academic environment shaped by the university model, can be tempted to teach our subjects in a dry, rationalistic manner with barely a trace of that awe and wonder that once led us into theological study in the first place. In his book, *Resting on the Heart of Christ: The Vocation and Spirituality of the Seminary Theologian*,[11] Deacon James Keating invites seminary faculty to prepare and present their lectures to "enflame pastoral desire" within the seminarians. As seminary faculty heed this call, they will assist seminarians to avoid the compartmentalization of theological study and its separation from prayer and worship.

Yet, despite the best efforts of his professors, the seminarian may still be tempted to compartmentalize theological study. The very rigor of the intellectual task involved in this study can lead to compartmentalization. Any sort of academic study is difficult, but theological study places additional demands on the student. The seminarian is asked to exert the effort to interpret the biblical sources, to grasp the historical developments, to master philosophical and theological vocabulary, to engage with contemporary challenges, and to recognize pastoral implications of each dogmatic formulation. It is easy to lose the awe and wonder in the midst of that intellectual labor and to lose the connection between dogma and doxology—hence, the need to build bridges between dogma and doxology, between theological study and prayer.

We will begin by considering how to build a bridge from prayer to study, from doxology to dogma. How does the seminarian carry with him the awe and wonder of the mystery experienced in prayer into his study of that mystery in the classroom? Then, we will consider how to build a bridge in the opposite direction. How does the seminarian take what he is learning in the classroom and carry that back to his prayer?

Building a Bridge from Doxology to Dogma: Wonder and Wondering

St. Anselm famously defined theology as "faith seeking understanding" and just as famously went on to ask "*Cur Deus homo?*" ("Why did God become man?"). His love and devotion to Christ (most evident when we read his prayers) led him to the rigorous and extensive questioning that drives his analysis of the Incarnation in *Cur Deus Homo*. The "wonder" of his prayer led him into the intellectual "wondering" of his treatise. St. Anselm illustrates the two senses of wonder and how both are essential to building this bridge from doxology to dogma. His prayers illustrate wonder understood as "a sense of surprising awe and admiration for some object of beauty or majesty."[12] In a prayer to the Cross, St. Anselm exclaims "O Cross to be *wondered* at . . . working of mercy and wisdom."[13] Anselm's theological treatises illustrate "wonder" in the sense of "the desire to know something, to be curious about something." St. Anselm begins his treatise *Cur Deus Homo* by wondering why "God became man" and "by his own death" restored us to life.[14] Using his dialogue partner "Boso" to ask question after question, Anselm wonders: Why did God become man? Why did He not just free us from the devil by force? Why did He die? Why is the repentance of the sinner not sufficient to make up for past sins? Why, of the three Persons of the Trinity, was it the Son who became Man? Why was He born of a virgin? (Anselm also poses many other questions along the way, about humans and angels, about human sin and

God's honor, about the demands of justice and the triumphs of mercy.

The awe and wonder that St. Anselm felt before the Mystery of the Incarnation and the Paschal Mystery led him to wonder why and how this mystery is suited to our need for salvation as sinful human beings. This wonder, expressed in his prayers, produced the wondering, the questioning, the exploration of the dogmas of Incarnation and Atonement in his theology. This tradition is obviously carried forward in the very structure of St. Thomas's questions, objections, and replies in the *Summa Theologica*. In more recent times (just to give a few examples), St. Pope John Paul II wondered about the meaning of human suffering in *Salvifici Doloris*; Pope Emeritus Benedict wondered how the hope of redemption can change our lives today in *Spe Salvi*; Pope Francis wonders what the doctrine of creation has to say to the current environmental crisis in *Laudato Si*.

Seminarians should feel free to wonder, to ask questions, to explore the "what?" the "why?" and the "how?" of God's works and God's ways. Seminarians often feel a hesitancy about such questioning. It seems like doubt. Questioning is associated with dissent, with heresy. Granted, there is a sort of questioning that rises out of unbelief, that questions only to challenge. However, that is not the only sort of questioning—as Anselm, Aquinas, and our recent popes illustrate. Seminarians need to feel freedom to ask questions from a place of trust. They will move from worship to study as they have the courage to acquire a holy curiosity that asks questions as a way of exploring the meaning and implications of revealed truths in a spirit of faith that combines wonder and wondering.

It is essential that the seminarian grow in this freedom for faithful wondering for two reasons. First, the seminarian must learn to enter empathetically into the questions and objections that our culture raises against the truths of faith. Pope Benedict characteristically associated theology with the exhortation in 1 Peter 3:15 to be always ready to give an answer (defense, apologia) to those who ask.[15] The seminarian needs encouragement to be a missionary disciple who desires to explore fully the questions that our post-Christian missionary field is asking that he might charitably and pastorally respond to those questions as one who has personally struggled through to answers.[16]

Secondly, the seminarian needs to have the courage to face the doubts, questions, and uncertainties in his own heart. The fear of facing his own questions creates a barrier that bars the seminarian from wondering and exploring the faith. He is tempted to approach Dogmatic theology as the mere memorization of ready-made answers and because he refuses to ask any questions, he never experiences the joy of wondering and exploring the breadths and depths of those answers. Worse, he fails to bring his own hidden doubts out into the light. By having the courage to wonder, to ask, to explore, seminarians learn to open their doubts to the healing power of God's truth. As they allow wonder to lead to wondering, seminarians will not only bridge the divide from doxology to dogma, they will experience theological study as a source of healing.

Building Bridges from Dogma to Doxology: Denzinger as a Prayerbook

Wonder that leads to wondering can move the seminarian from prayer into study of the mysteries of faith. What about the reverse direction? How can the seminarian carry the dogmas he studies in class into his doxological encounter with God in prayer?

Sooner or later in his studies of dogmatic theology, the seminarian will become acquainted with that indispensable collection of magisterial texts known eponymously by its original compiler, Heinrich Joseph Dominicus Denzinger. Thanks to Ignatius Press, we finally have an up-to-date English translation of *A Compendium of Creeds, Definitions, and Declarations on Matters of Faith and Morals*.[17] This work is typically used as a reference book, a place to locate authoritative statements on a specific dogma. It can easily be used as a weapon, a repository of texts to throw at heretics, both real and imagined. In fact, Karl Rahner (who himself served as an editor for several editions of Denzinger) warned against "Denzinger theology," a simplistic use of the anthology as a source of proof-texts without a careful contextual understanding of the material. Still, when used properly, Denzinger provides a place to learn the language of faith, to study the mysteries of faith, the dogmas of our religion in the very language with which Mother Church defines them. Yet, this language—with its definitions, distinctions (and condemnations)—can seem somewhat distant from the doxological language we learn from the Liturgy and prayer.

How might the seminarian take the language of dogmatic definitions and make it the language of prayer? How can the seminarian take these dogmas as they are explained in class, discussed in his textbooks, defined in sources like Denzinger, and make them a source of prayer, of meditation, of dialogue and communion with the Holy Trinity? As I did with *lectio* and exegesis above, I want to propose a simple practice that can be very fruitful in helping the seminarian build a bridge from dogmatic study to doxological prayer. I developed this practice as a result of reading an article about the council of Chalcedon and its dogmatic definition on the two natures of Christ.[18] In this essay, patristic scholar John McGuckin emphasizes that the early creeds were often adapted from ancient baptismal confessions. They are derived from pre-existing liturgical and sacramental language. While we tend to think of creeds as doctrinal summaries, they are better understood in light of their origins, as doxological confessions of praise. In response to the needs of the times, certain anathemas or condemnations of heretical opinions are added to these confessions of faith, thereby obscuring their original doxological character. Toward the end of his essay, McGuckin re-presents the words of the Chalcedonian definition (minus the anathemas) as a way of uncovering the doxological core of this dogmatic definition. At the core of this dogmatic definition, McGuckin finds a doxological "prayer to the savior."

This set me to thinking about doing something similar with other creedal, conciliar, and papal definitions of dogma. Could I use Denzinger as a prayer book? For example, could I take the dogmatic definitions of Trinitarian dogma, such as we find in the Nicene Creed, in the ancient Councils of Toledo, and the so-called Athanasian Creed and make them prayers to the Father, Son, and Spirit? It proves quite easy to change "I believe in God the Father" to "I believe in *You*, God the Father." To take each phrase of a dogmatic definition, to pause and meditate on it as a statement about God and then to speak it back in a personal way as a prayer to God provides a simple bridge between dogmatic study and doxological prayer.

I would encourage a seminarian to take key magisterial texts related to the dogmas he is studying in class that semester, and take some time to pray with those texts. The seminarian should meditate on those texts and re-phrase them to make them personal prayers to God. For example, part of the Chalcedonian definition reads as follows:

> We unanimously teach and confess one and the same Son, our Lord Jesus Christ: the same perfect in divinity and perfect in humanity, the same truly God and truly man, composed of rational soul and body; consubstantial with the Father as to his divinity and consubstantial with us as to his humanity; "like us in all things but sin."

The seminarian can restate that text as a prayer. For example:

I confess *You* are one and the same Son, our

Lord Jesus Christ: *You* are perfect in divinity and perfect in humanity, *You* are truly God and truly man, composed of rational soul and body; *You* are consubstantial with the Father as to your divinity and consubstantial with us (with *me*) as to your humanity; "like us in all things but sin."

Now, the fourteen-hundred-plus-page volume of Denzinger published in Latin and English might be a hefty volume to lug into chapel for one's holy hour. *The Christian Faith* is a shorter English translation of these magisterial texts that has the added benefit of grouping the magisterial documents topically, rather than chronologically—as Denzinger does.[19] A seminarian can use that collection to meditate and pray with key magisterial texts on the specific dogmas he is studying that semester easily gathered together in one place. Of course, in a digital format, these sources become quite accessible on one's tablet or phone. A seminarian can do the same thing with the *Catechism of the Catholic Church.* The way it blends dogmatic definitions with copious quotations from Scripture, Church Fathers, and saints, the Catechism readily lends itself to this sort of meditation and prayer.

The dogmas seminarians study in their classes are not apprehended by intellect alone. They do demand study and rigorous thought, but they are mysteries to be received in prayer and contemplated with the heart. How beneficial it would be if a seminarian had not only studied all the required dogmas in his classes, but alongside each class, he had taken some time to receive those dogmas in prayer and meditation and had actually prayed those dogmas back to the Father, to the Son, and to the Spirit as his personal confession of faith, his words of praise and adoration. I think he would carry these dogmas, these mysteries in his heart. They would be more than "facts" he learned in class. They would be places of encounter with God. They would be truths he eagerly desires to share with the flock that will someday, God willing, be entrusted to his pastoral care.

Building a Bridge between the Classroom and Spiritual Direction

If the seminarian adopts these and other practices of his own to build bridges between exegesis and *lectio*, between dogma and doxology, he will make great strides toward overcoming compartmentalization and integrating his intellectual and spiritual formation. However, the most crucial bridge that needs to be built is one that overcomes the divide between the classroom and spiritual direction. This may be where compartmentalization can be at its greatest. Of course, with spiritual direction, we are talking about a confidential relationship, the internal forum. So, I cannot know what is discussed there. But I wonder: Does the seminarian regularly talk to his spiritual director about the mysteries of faith he is studying in his classes? Does he bring to spiritual direction questions that these classes raise? I do not mean intellectual questions that the professor can answer after class, but more personal questions around receiving these truths and allowing them to touch the heart with their transformative power. The truths of our faith are transformative. It could be the spiritual director who helps the seminarian tap into the transformation power of the truths he is studying in class.

The classroom can be a place of spiritual illumination and even spiritual healing. For example, one can imagine a situation where a seminarian struggles to receive God's love for him. He thinks he needs to work to earn God's favor instead of receiving Divine love as a gift. The spiritual director provides some good counsel but to no avail. Then, the seminarian takes a class on "Sin and Grace." He recognizes some of his own false thinking in the heresies of Pelagianism and Jansenism. He grasps the Good News of the Gospel in a new way. The professor's explanation of grace becomes a moment of illumination. This scenario will reach its full potential as the seminarian shares these newfound intellectual insights with his spiritual director. The classroom provided the spiritual medicine the seminarian needed. The spiritual director can very carefully apply that medicine to those specific wounds the seminarian has revealed within the safety of their relationship.

It may not be as dramatic as this imagined scenario, but if seminarians regularly shared with their spiritual directors some of the insights (and questions) coming from their coursework, they would more fully realize the transformative potential of the truths they are learning in class, and they would go far toward a fuller integration of their spiritual and intellectual formation.

All the above are simple practices, attempts to overcome compartmentalization by building bridges between bifurcated dimensions of seminary formation. Ultimately, it is the grace of the Holy Spirit who will enable the seminarian to use these practices or other practices toward a rich integration of his human, spiritual, intellectual, and pastoral formation.

NOTES

1. United States Conference of Catholic Bishops (USCCB), *Program of Priestly Formation*, 5th ed. (Washington DC: USCCB, 2006), sec. 82.

2. Ibid., sec. 115.

3. Ibid., sec. 164.

4. Ibid., sec. 241.

5. Ibid., sec. 136.

6. Benedict XVI, *Verbum Domini* (2010), sec. 35.

7. Benedict XVI, *Jesus of Nazareth* (San Francisco: Ignatius Press, 2008), xv.

8. Francis, *Evangelii Gaudium* (2013), sec. 146-148.

9. Ibid., sec. 149, citing John Paul II, *Pastores Dabo Vobis* (1992), sec. 26.

10. *Evangelii Gaudium*, sec. 152.

11. James Keating, *Resting on the Heart of Christ: The Vocation and Spirituality of the Seminary Theologian* (Omaha: IPF Publications, 2009).

12. *Prayers and Meditations of Saint Anselm,* trans. Benedicta Ward (Harmondsworth: Penguin, 1973).

13. Ibid.

14. *Cur Deus Homo*, I.1. "The question on which the whole work rests."

15. See, for example, Joseph Cardinal Ratzinger, *Nature and Mission of Theology* (San Francisco: Ignatius Press, 1995), 26.

16. Christopher Collins, S.J. develops this theme in "Doubt and the Task of Theology in the New Evangelization," *Entering into the Mind of Christ*, ed. James Keating (Omaha, NE: IPF Publications, 2014).

17.   Heinrich Joseph Denzinger, *A Compendium of Creeds, Definitions, and Declarations on Matters of Faith and Morals*, ed. Peter Hunermann (San Francisco: Ignatius Press, 2012).

18.   See John A. McGuckin, "Mystery or Conundrum? The Apprehension of Christ in the Chalcedonian Definition," *In the Shadow of the Incarnation: Essays on Jesus Christ in the Early Church in Honor of Brian Daley, S.J.*, ed. Peter Martens (Notre Dame, IN: University of Notre Dame Press, 2008).

19.   J. Dupuis, S.J. and J. Neuner, S.J., *The Christian Faith in the Doctrinal Documents of the Catholic Church*, ed. Jacques Dupuis (New York: Alba House, 1996).